To Cyri

with warm regards
[illegible]
12/3.2000

THE REMNANT

THE REMNANT

Poems by

Simcha Simchovitch

With an Introduction by Raymond Souster

Mosaic Press
TORONTO PARIS NEW YORK

Canadian Cataloguing in Publication Data

Simchovitch, S. (Sam), 1921-
The remnant

Poems.
ISBN 0-88962-697-9

I. Title

PS8537.I51R45 1999 C811'.54 C99-930433-X
PR9199.3.S55R45 1999

Published by MOSAIC PRESS, P.O. Box 1032, Oakville, Ontario, L6J 5E9, Canada. Offices and warehouse at 1252 Speers Road, Units #1&2, Oakville, Ontario, L6L 5N9, Canada and Mosaic Press, 85 River Rock Drive, Suite 202, Buffalo, N.Y., 14207, USA.

Mosaic Press acknowledges the assistance of the Canada Council and the Department of Canadian Heritage, Government of Canada, for their support of our publishing programme.

THE CANADA COUNCIL FOR THE ARTS SINCE 1957 | LE CONSEIL DES ARTS DU CANADA DEPUIS 1957

ISBN 0-88962- 697-9

Printed and bound in Canada

MOSAIC PRESS, in Canada:
1252 Speers Road, Units #1&2, Oakville, Ontario, L6L 5N9
Phone / Fax: (905) 825-2130
E-mail: cp507@freenet.toronto.on.ca

MOSAIC PRESS, in the USA:
85 River Rock Drive, Suite 202, Buffalo, N.Y., 14207
Phone / Fax: 1-800-387-8992
E-mail: cp507@freenet.toronto.on.ca

ACKNOWLEDGMENTS

I express my sincere thanks to the esteemed Canadian poet Raymond Souster for reading the manuscript and providing the short but succinct Introduction. I am also indepted to the poets Kenneth Sherman and Sylvia Warsh for their valuable suggestions, as well as to Fay Kellerstein for translating a number of poems from the Yiddish original.

As before, my gratitude goes to the distinguished patrons of the arts Joseph B. and Olyn Horwitz of Cleveland, Ohio, and Izzy and Betty Kirshenbaum of Toronto who generously support all my publications. Warm thanks are also due to Dr. Fred and Joy Weinberg. Milton and Joyce Shier, Israel Kopyto, Victor and René Topper and the Beth Tzededc congregation for their encouragement and contributions.

Simcha Simchovitch

TABLE OF CONTENTS

I. THERE

II. MY BRETHREN

III. MY SONG

INTRODUCTION

Right from the opening pages of Sam Simchovitch's new collection of poems, mainly translations of his Yiddish writings, I was struck by their overwhelming burden of anger and remorse. Anger toward the oppressors and their easy abandonment of all common decency, expressionless robots going through their slaughter-house routines; remorse that as a young boy he was powerless to lift a finger to help in any way his loved ones and the neighbours of his town. No one should have to carry a load like this on their shoulders for even a short time, but Sam Simchovitch has done it for these many years, as Paul Celan did, as Nelly Sachs did, as Tadeusz Rozewicz did. Now his voice rings out as one of the very last of the survivors – and it is a voice we should listen to and learn from, if it is not already too late...

I salute Sam Simchovitch as one fellow poet to another. My only hope now is that he may be allowed a chance to reach a wider audience he so richly deserves.

Toronto, 1998 Raymond Souster

I.
THERE

THERE

There my life unfolded.
With all my senses I absorbed
my Jewish world in Poland,
before it was defiled and erased
in six ghastly years
of blood-inundation and Divine eclipse.

Alive and effervescent in me
are words and songs of my people
in streets and in homes,
in studyhouses, worker's unions,
joy at weddings, circumcisions,
before disaster like an avalanche descended
upon our Sabbaths and our weekdays.

Arise, my sunken continent,
from the sea of forgetfulness
in your comely poverty,
in your enormous solitude!
Let my memory recall
familiar names, forms and features
of dear ones, friends and comrades
confined in ghettos, death-camps,
hiding in cellars, in the woods.

And let the tears of commiseration flow
from the very depth of my being.

Translated by Faye Kellerstein

TO YOU

I soaked in your sadness and mirth
like the earth absorbs blessed rain;
I was drunk with sighs and sorrows
of my courtyard and lane.

Your celebrations, your woes
have permeated all my songs;
bound and eternally betrothed,
to you I belong.

MY TREASURY

Like some heaven sent treasury
I carry my home in my memory.

I hear those familiar lullabies,
laughter, and tears, and cries.

I see all that lively, blossoming youth,
the dreamers, the seekers of justice and truth.

The streets resounded with the ring of their song,
and I among them, alive and young.

How it could happen, I can't comprehend
that everything came to such a dire end.

Those ruined homes, those battered streets stare
like frightful ghosts, deformed and bare.

And I, the spared one, commiserate
through the veil of years, their undeserved fate.

YOM KIPPUR NIGHTS

Alive in my memory are *Yom Kippur* nights
in my hometown, Otwock, Poland.
The sky there was dark and dreary,
and a somber stillness hovered around
as if the entire world held its breath
in awe before the Day of Judgment.

In prayerhouses congregations
gathered, in holy reverence
before the One who lives eternally
and weighs the deeds of all on this day.
The tall *Yahrzeit* candles flickered
like the hearts of the assembled men,
the tallow dripping into boxes of sand
like warm tears from the women's eyes.

In a corner, Father, wrapped in his *tallis*,
was beating his fist on his chest
in solemn confession of the *Al Chet*;
and in the women's gallery
Mother poured her heart out before the One Above
in prayer for her five little doves.

HASIDIM

Semi-darkness covers the prayer room,
the Sabbath departs, the weekdays are here,
the heart is sunken in grief and anguish
for days of greyness, need and fear.

Hasidim sit quietly, subdued in thought,
some sigh deeply, "*Oy vey! Oy vey!*"
Another one, pacing back and forth,
takes leave of the cherished Sabbath day.

Suddenly a young fellow, tall and lean,
begins a tune, first shyly and slow;
others join in, it's a new *nigun*
the *rebbe* composed not long ago.

Soon all rise and arm in arm
unite in an enchanted chain;
they rise and fall, exalted
in fiery circles, again and again.

The *rebbe's* eyes beam with joy,
a sweet smile plays on his gentle face.
"A good week to you, my fellow Jews,
may *Shaddai* bless you with His goodness and grace."

OUR HOME

Our one-room is cold and damp,
lit by a meagre electric lamp.
In the middle stands a table, battered,
three wobbly chairs, an old taboret.
In the makeshift kitchen mother stands
by the faltering fire, with her tired, chapped hands
a few potatoes and carrots she peels,
nourishment for our evening meal.
By the window, beside the first bed,
Father sits, from morning to sunset,
at his old leather stitching noisy machine,
this – his daily solemn routine.
Mother brings the soup to the table,
sighing each time she dips the ladle.
After the meal I retreat to a nook
to spend some time with a favourite book.
Outside, at night, the raw wind blows,
it rattles frames and threatens every window.
Father recites his prayers for the night,
he lies in bed, my little brother at his side.
Asleep, my two sisters hold one another
in the second bed, beside my tired mother.
I make for my folding cot by the door,
cold creeps up from beneath the floor
and penetrates my sagging bed.
Our days are bound by a pitch-dark thread.

MY FATHER

My father was a proud, honest Jew.
His eyes shone with the distilled wisdom
of many tested, holy generations.
Sure and faithful were his steps.

Deep were his words, even more his silence.
He carried life's heavy burden
calmly and modestly, without complaint
or bittnerness towards his Maker.

Six children filled our one-room home,
he alone was their provider;
in winter often need and want broke in
like enraged and hungry beasts.

But my father drove them from our home
With the droning of his sewing-machine.
He consoled himself: For sure there must be
meaning and justice in God's world.

When the fires of war were ablaze
and I abandoned our endangered nest,
he remained with my mother and the children
to protect them from fear and hunger.

And when they led the town's Jews away
through panicked and pogromed streets,
he walked beside his children quietly
toward the Treblinka-destined cattle cars.

SEPARATION

The train filled to bursting
with refugees torn from warm homes,
loving parents, wives and children.
Pangs of guilt filled my heart
as though I was abandoning
a burning house or a ship
shortly before its sinking.
I was leaving behind
Father, Mother, three younger sisters,
and a dear little brother.
An hour or two before
when I had said farewell
both to them and the neighbours
gathered in our courtyard,
Mother had wept over me,
flung her arms around my neck
and embraced me -
her eldest son, her *Kaddish*.
The siblings, all in tears, followed suit,
neighbours clasped my hands.
Only Father remained silent.
Handing me a ten-zloty bill,
he whispered,
"Remember us, Simche, remember!"

Translated by Faye Kellerstein

REFUGEES

Our train trudges slowly, unsurely,
the sky is transparent and clear,
then a squadron of German planes
suddenly appears on the horizon.

The train grinds to a halt, we scurry
into the forest by the tracks.
Above us Messerschmidts circle
and fire their deadly bullets.

I fall and embrace a tree trunk,
a Pole beside me cries, "*Ola Boga!*"
A miracle happens – the planes are gone,
the refugees safe for a while.

We run back to our empty coaches,
the train trudges slowly on again
over this fair land which the hordes
are trampling with their boots and swords.

MOTHER

From afar I call to you,
and everywhere I hear your sobbing.
Would that I had wings to fly
over all the barriers of years back to you!

I see you on the doorstep of our home,
a bent and solitary willow.
You walk with me, Mother,
yours tears burn in my very bones.

Translated by Faye Kellerstein

MY MOTHER'S LETTER

My son, my crown, my *Kaddish* sayer,
sole consolation of my life,
my eyes were dry, no more tears would come
until I heard your words "I am alive!"
Then I knew that God had heard my pleas
and delivered your warm greetings to me.

Take care, my child, do not worry,
the time of our trials will pass,
hopefully we'll survive
until you'll return, well and alive.
Thus I pray day and night
to the One who is always right.

IN AN ALIEN LAND

High overhead the sun shines down upon me,
encouraging me on my journey.
Already behind me is the mountain village
I left at dawn, never to return.
I descend on mountain paths
beside dizzying precipices,
and see my reflection in the clear water
of the fast flowing Sir-Daria River.
Soon I will wash the dust
off my hands and face
in the coolness of that stream.

I press on further. Behind me
the mountain peaks of Kirghizia.
Before me – a wide open valley
with bronze waving cornstalks.
I cover the distance quickly,
approach a new village.
Over the clay huts smoke swirls,
dogs bark behind hedges and fences.

O I walk and walk, a castaway
in a sun-flooded alien land.

Translated by Faye Kellerstein

MY FRIEND IS DYING

Huddled in the shade of a fence of clay
to escape the raging, blistering sun,
my friend is dying, far-away from home,
in a strange and foreign land.

Together we had studied and aspired
to achieve much in our young lives
in the land of the Worker's Soviets
where we found a refuge in wartime.

Soon we had to flee once more. The Nazi scourge
sent his hordes into Russia's lands.
By war-time trains we made our way
deep south, into sunny Kirghizstan.

Here we suffered hunger, homelessness,
then, in hospital, the typhus ravaged him,
until he curled upon on the soft, hot ground,
to die in the shade of this fence of clay.

THE LAST NIGHT

"But for Thy sake we were killed
all day long, we were considered
like sheep led to slaughter."
(Ps. 44:23)

Night...
A Jewish town sways in delirium
like flocks of sheep
without guardians or shepherds.
People plead and cry
in terrifying amazement,
while feet drag on, entangled
in the dark nets of death.
Only somewhere, deep inside,
a ray of hope smolders:
a dream of survival.

Menachem-Mendel, recluse and mystic,
darts from Otwock *Rebbe's* courtyard
along the ghetto's main street.
The tails of his gaberdine like black wings
flutter on both sides. He clasps
his shriveled hands and calls:
"*Gevald, Yiddn!* Do not despair!"

No one hears him. Over the ghetto lanes
panic rises like a threatening cloud,
an epidemic that quickly penetrates
house after house in the area.
Each household is awake
with sobs and feverish talk.
They pack bundles, rucksacks,
tie the rumpled bedding,
bury previous heirlooms,
the Sabbath candleholders, menorahs,
beloved objects of heritage
passed down from mothers, grandmothers.

Beside piles of pillows, featherbeds,
the drowsy children lie completely dressed.
They know everything: Tomorrow
they will all be taken
into a dark, unknown land.
No more will they crawl under
the barbed wire of the ghetto fence,
to the fields along Vistula's shores,
to dig out a few potatoes, radishes,
for their hungry parents and siblings
who will thank them and pat them lovingly.

Fathers, like dark gravediggers,
venture outside into ghetto streets.
They gather in groups on corners,
they sway, gesticulate like shadows,
they beg, one from another,
any shred of consolation.
"What is happening?
Where can one hide or flee?
They say we are destined
for a place of no return..."

Binyomin the Butcher, who on market days
used to beat up Polish drunks
when they bothered Jewish merchants,
walks among the assembled men
with his butcher axe in his belt.
"Jews," he calls in his hoarse voice,
"we are lost anyway!
Tomorrow we will be led to death
just as I was leading my cows and calves
into the slaughterhouse.
Jews, take iron bars, hammers, axes
sharpen your tailor scissors, cobbler knives,
and when the murderers arrive in the morning,
do not stand like clay dummies,
but strike straight into their filthy snouts!"
Thus he yelped like a wounded animal
while all around fell silent.

Dawn...
Fathers, mothers and children
doze on sacks and bundles.
Others lie in hiding places
alone, awake for hours,
with hearts shrunken, in cold sweat,
counting the hours and minutes.

Suddenly ...
The earth trembles with the boom of motors,
the air is pierced with rifle salvos,
sirens howl, announcing
the final hour of the ghetto.

And with a curse on their lips,
eight thousand Jews are led
to the freight-trains for Treblinka.

THE REMNANT

After eight thousand Otwock Jews
were sent to their deaths in Treblinka,
some four thousand more remained in hiding.
Day by day they were traced, discovered
in attics, cellars of the empty ghetto.
Others came out themselves from hiding
driven by hunger, thirst and despair.
They walked together in gloomy silence
to the ghetto police station.

Upon the ground, in a wire enclosure,
guarded by their own Jewish policemen,
mothers and children sat squeezed together,
father and sons, young and old.
Some cried to Heaven, even deplored
the Almighty who has no pity
on infants and youths, lovely daughters.
Others sang pensive Yiddish folk songs,
Yom Kippur prayers, chapters of Psalms,
recalled aloud their former good deeds
or regretted their life-long thrift
to save for a rainy day somewhere in the future.
The children beside them sat silent and humble,
crying no more for food or drink.

Twice a week, early in the morning,
ten German gendarmes arrived.
With them were Polish policemen
and behind – the Judenrat's guardsmen
with caps and armbands, truncheons in hands.
One by one the Germans entered
the fenced area of the doomed Jews,
demanding jewellery, money and gold.

Men and women knelt in front of them
as if before ancient, monstrous gods.
They handed over hidden possessions –
wedding rings, watches, earrings, money,
imploring mercy for their offspring,
the fruit of their loins and wombs.

A team of grave diggers arrived,
Jewish inmates from the camp in nearby Karczew.
Hurriedly they were told to dig
a deep wide pit with a heaped up sandhill.
Now the gendarmes began to drive
the first ten Jews from the enclosure.
Some hurried through the short distance,
some held tightly each others' hands,
others walked slowly, silent, proud,
or cursed aloud the murderous race.
Now at the sandhill they were forced
to lie face-down upon the clear sand.
Then came the order, the fiery salvos,
and bullets smashed heads and backs.
Here the Karczew inmates were ordered
to shovel the bodies into the pit.

The sandhill was cleared now, ready and waiting
for another lot of Jews,
blameless as the clear morning
that shone through the tall pines
of the Otwock villas around them.
Not far away from the mass grave
stood the Germans, combat boots shining,
the sweat dripping from beneath their helmets,
they hurriedly gulped from beer bottles,
engrossed in the slaughter of the remnant Jews.

And further on, behind wired fences,
a crowd of townspeople was assembled,
to witness the unholy spectacle
of the final end to the Otwock Jews.

Rested from a night's sleep, having taken breakfast,
women in light summer dresses,
men in short sleeves, in summer hats.
Many of them will now inherit
Jewish homes and their possessions,
their children will play freely
in Jewish courtyards, villas, streets;
their maidens will adorn themselves
in the wool and in silk of Jewish daughters;
erased forever will be the memory
of all who lived here, laboured hard to build
such a fine resort town.

From afar they may have distinguished
former neighbours, colleagues, friends.
Here walks to her death, Yentl, the pretty daughter
of Isaac Mokotowski, the wealthy merchant,
owner of a brick house beside the bazaar.
Her sister-in-law walks bravely beside her,
both lovely women in the prime of life.
Only two days ago they both took refuge
in the ghetto police station,
trusting that there they would be safe.
Next morning, Kronenberg, Commandant
of the ghetto's police detachment,
drove them into the wired enclosure.
(The Germans will later shoot him, too.
together with Tola, his pampered wife.)
Now both Mokotowski women hurry,
hand in hand to their destination,
at the golden sandhill they quickly embrace
and under the hail of bullets,
roll together into the mass grave.

And so the annihilation continued,
twice a week,
in August - September 1942,
in the midst of the Second World War.
... And the Jews of Otwock were no more.

AUGUST 19, 1942

My home is on fire, from afar I hear
the calls for help, the cries of despair.
The sky is azure, bright is the sun,
but they are silent, they only look on
how Einsatz-men, with murderous lust,
drive and chase the blameless and just
with truncheons, pistols, with rifle butts,
with devilish laughter and fiendish shouts.
Fathers and mothers surrounded by kids,
the old, the feeble lost in their midst.
On to the rail-station, like animal freight,
to lead them away into hellish gates.

At night, in the ghetto, each window and door
gape like skeletons after a war.
Shadows like spectres scurry around
like beasts fleeing a murderous hunt.
They creep out of hiding and find none
of their close ones, all are gone.
What is there to live for, what is the gain
when none of your dearest did remain?!
They give themselves up, in desperation,
into the Judenrat's police station.
In an enclosure, under the sky,
two or three days there they'll stay
until the German gendearmes arrive
to end the remnant's lives.

My home is no more, no one was spared,
alone I remain on gruesome earth;
alone with the memory of the guiltless and pure,
alone to go on and endure.

FAMILY PHOTOGRAPH

My six innocent souls,
you were mercilessly uprooted
and painfully cut down
while I alone was spared.

You look at me, silent and gentle,
from the dark family photograph
on the wall of my study.
When I see you, I'm back
in our poor nest in Poland
before the evil ones emptied it,
hurtling me to all the winds,
that I may carry your images
like holy tablets.

And until my last breath
mourn and bevail you.

Translated by Faye Kellerstein

ON THAT DAY

The last fires are blazing in the streets,
my home is drowning in a sea of blood.
The wings of flames carry and scatter
the last cries of agony and despair.

The world is silent, dumbstruck at the carnage,
the earth did not shudder nor move
from its orbit,
the heaven did not split asunder;
God himself hid his face, in panic,
on that day.

Translated by Faye Kellerstein

WARSAW GHETTO

Swollen bodies clutch the ground,
hungry eyes pierce the silent sky;
a street musician conjures sad tunes
of a ghetto lullaby.

Barefoot children wrapped in rags
sing with voices, clear and thin,
the swan song of the Warsaw ghetto
on cold and grimy pavements.

GHETTO HEROES

In the glare of the huge ghetto pyre
that consumed all, root and stem,
they pronounced such a solemn vow:
"No more to die like a silent lamb!"

But with fire and with scorching steel
defend each bunker and each ghetto lane
against the slayers, intoxicated
with Jewish blood and pain.

IN GHETTO RUINS

Eternal autumn, dreary rain,
pours on ruined ghetto lanes,
among frozen mounds, raw and bare,
remnants of the Jewish quarter stare.

A torn prayerbook, amidst clods of earth,
cries into the gloomy night unheard.
The wind picks up its woeful lament
and carries it into the ravaged ferment
that suddenly begins to boil and seethe
like waves on a stormy sea.
And all the heaps of rubble cry:
"Why?!"

THE FIDDLER OF BIRKENAU

Thus he played, the fiddler,
of Auschwitz-Birkenau,
when with marches he accompanied
the emaciated work-gangs
in striped rags, with numbers
burned into their arms.

Now, a half century later,
he stands before a gathering of survivors
and plays again his fiddle,
tunes thin and somber –
a memorial for those
who did not live to see and hear.

WHO WOULD GUESS

Who would guess that my neighbour,
a Jew in his eighties,
who walks slowly each morning
three miles along the highway
beside our summer resort,
who would know: He is a hero
who outsmarted the German henchmen
and their bloodthirsty local minions
in the town of Stryj, in the Ukraine.

He prepared a hideout
with running water and provisions.
Though his wife and child were snatched
in the first day of the ghetto action,
he, with his older son, reached the bunker.

Long days and nights, for eighteen months,
in the damp, darkened cellar,
the small band of Jews survived,
men, women and children.
Equally they shared the meagre food rations,
quieted the children, solaced one another,
counted the days, dreamed
of outliving the executioners.

Inscribed with golden letters be the names
of two faithful Polish neighbours
who guarded the hidden Jews
and provided their daily bread.

ZYGMUND SOBOLEWSKI

Zygmund Sobolewski,
in striped Auschwitz outfit,
lifts his arms toward heaven,
pleads forgiveness
from the murdered Jews of Poland.

He recalls the days of toil and drudgery,
the barking dogs, their spiked teeth
menacing from the open snouts,
the murderous growl of the guards,
the lashes upon naked bodies.

He still smells
cremated human flesh,
still sees
the huddled mothers and children
waiting their turn
into the gas chambers.

And he asks, "Where was humanity?
Why did so many by the wayside stay
and look on, with indifference,
even satisfaction,
as waves of human misery and pain
were beating on their doors and gates?!"

Zygmund Sobolewski, Auschwitz number 88.
His oldest son will tattoo it
on his right arm and carry
his father's testimony – the memory
of souls who flutter without end
asking for remembrance and atonement.

THE GATHERER
For Hanna Krall

Toiling incessantly, she gathers mementos
from those years of the great lament
when millions were dispatched to their end.

Neat and gentle, with womanly grace,
she rummages in attics, dark holes,
for echoes of those cries and calls.

From under dust of time she digs
bits and pieces of testimony –
from fathers, sons and their progeny.

Here and there she finds a soul
yearning for its root and stem –
and shares tears with them.

THE HEALING WORD
For Donia Blumenfeld Clenman

Out of the abyss of fire and sword,
you carried the precious, healing word

Of love and pain – a compassioned cry
to all who breathe under God's sky.

You dreamt in good English, too,
of hidden scars and buried woe,

but spread your arms to embrace
Humanity – of every colour and race.

TWENTIETH CENTURY

The whiteness of snow, the sun's golden glare,
the bursting joy, lament of despair,
the cry of the newborn, and of the undone
in battles lost, in onslaughts won;
the innocent day and the searing hate
that flows in the ether, and suffocates;
the grandiose idol – atomic bliss,
back off, humanchild, at the edge of Abyss.

THUS A YOUTH PERISHED

There youths grew up and blossomed,
I see them through the fog of decades.
In the streets and lanes of Poland
rustled a young Jewish forest.

How can I forget the glimmer in eyes
of those who dreamt of world redemption?
Their brave hearts throbbed with longings
like eagles aspiring into wide horizons.

Till now I'm followed by Horah dances,
when hands entwine in ecstatic sway,
and lives elevate in fiery circles
higher and higher on rungs of mirth.

There were *"Shomrim"*, free and reckless,
who left their homes in cities and towns.
Sunburnt, they wandered on Polish roads
with songs of Zion, with dashing steps.

I still hear the whisper at secret meetings,
in the dark grove on grass they rested;
the clamour of lively *Bundist* youth groups
solemnly singing the old-new "Oath".

Who can forget the fair, young maidens
like roses adorning each circle and group;
the couples who sauntered in dark alleys
to kiss under the radiant moon.

In towns where need cried out from doors,
they were the solace, the hope and joy,
but mothers wailed often when pavements
were stained with young blood of sons.

Enlightened by new mentors and teachings,
they undid and built the world anew,
and each one was anxious to find the right way
his own people and the world to set free.

And all of them fluttered with love and pity
for the worlds' downtrodden sisters and brothers;
they carried their lives forth on altars –
to the sands of the *Negev*, on streets of Madrid.

In Polish jails, caged behind bars,
they drank the gloom of the darkest cells;
they spit the blood on an unjust world
and expired like sparks in the dark.

They dried the swamps of the Huleh Valley
and stole the border to the Soviet "Eden";
they filled the streets of Jewish Poland
with lively unrest, clamour and song.

But when the dark hour of war arrived
they were abandoned, betrayed by all;
in vain they stretched their young arms
over ghetto walls and barbed wire.

Till the last they believed and hoped
in a tomorrow of sunshine and life,
till the flames enveloped, consumed
the whole generation, the young with the old.

Until the axes of the German slaughterers
cut down the forest, root and branch.
And a deadly silence befell the shtetls
of Poland and Lithuania.

II.
MY BRETHREN

MY BRETHREN

My heart is open in love
for you, my brethren
of Poland, Morocco, the Ukraine,
by the shores of the Hudson and Dnieper.

Mercurial are you, restless,
deep as the night is your sorrow,
glowing like sunshine is your joy.
I would know you in the dark
by the glimmer of your eyes,
by your hurried gait.
I follow you like a shadow
in capitals of many lands.

In new lands, overseas,
you regained your vigour,
your sons grew tall and daughters
blossomed like slender flowers.

No doubt they'll carry our heritage
in the adopted lands,
and there where eastern skies
pour sunshine into the veins
of our everlasting stem.

ODE TO MY HUMBLE BRETHREN

For Melech and Rachel Ravitch

With all my limbs, with my whole being,
like a tree rooted in black soil,
I am tied, linked to you –
my humble brethren.
    Like a child that clings to a mother's skirt,
    afraid to get lost and forlorn,
    I hold on tightly to you –
    my humble brethren.
Let the genteel sneer, put on airs,
to me agreeable is your sweat
and dear the grey days of toil –
my humble brethren.
    More than once I, too, have sinned
    with words of chastisement and frowning look,
    to wake you from your quietude –
    my humble brethren.
But now I'll take off my shoes
and cast away all words of reproof,
and like a penitent come to you –
my humble brethren.
    And sure I am that there I will find
    hidden sparks of the *Baal Shem*
    and the *Shechinah* nesting among you –
    my humble brethren.
And if some good is yet destined for me
on our sad and calloused earth,
I'd like to walk and sing among you –
my humble brethren.

THEY SAY

They say you have no base or substance,
you are fossilized cobweb and dust,
but in my blood runs your ancient vigour
and your living song – in my breast.

In front of you the turbulence of nations
and Pharaoh's chariots pursue from behind,
but you proceed, in fire proven and tested,
with Holy Writ eternally aligned.

The tired and perplexed fall by the wayside,
the road is long and the horizon red,
but generations rise to share your treasure trove
and renew the covenant – for life and death.

The heart is heavy and the eyes in tears
for the ravages of not long ago,
but my soul is still uplifted
by the eternal Sinaitic glow.

YIDDISH TONGUE

Wherever I go, I carry
the orphaned voices
of those who are no more –
my Yiddish language and lore.

I sucked it with mother's milk,
I drank it like daylight with my eyes,
I hearkened to it in pious sighs
of mothers, grandmothers.

O Yiddish language, mother tongue,
you are sweet like honey
and, like wormwood, bitter.
With you I have risen and fallen,
with you I mourn and sing,
in your pained letters I sink,
until my heartbeat will
stand suddenly still.

PRAYER OF A YIDDISH POET

Lord of song, hidden source
of truth and beauty in the universe,
you endowed me with the gift of poetry
of Yiddish song that blossomed
like on a tree after wintry snowdrifts,
perceive my prayer, my supplication:
Let my well bubble with living water
and refresh my palate with Yiddish words;
let my song honour and uplift me
and the fruitful days – last and multiply.

IN THE KINGDOM

For David Volpe

In the kingdom of beauty and sadness
I seek forgetfulness, elevation.
Against vanity lurking all over –
an anthem to life and to being.

In lines like silken tulle
that whisper with hidden enchantment,
like gentle and still lullabies –
against the infinity of fear.

Like light-blossoms the stars sprout
and sunbeams stroke and caress,
like hidden seeds that flourish –
the kernels of bards and poets.

Against the horror and madness
of murderous, unruly tribes –
odes of love and of mercy,
anthems of life and being.

IN VAIN

In the workshop, from morn to eve,
they follow me in dizzying review;
I fend them off, my own poems,
lest the needle stitch goes askew.

At home they lie, a pile of papers
with dark cursive Hebrew lines;
in them I stored my rare joy
and my hidden sighs and pains.

Should I tear them up, my writings,
like a mourner his attire,
free myself, like an inmate,
from these shackles, this barbed wire?

In vain are my pleadings,
and for naught my bitter strife;
the word will not abandon me,
it is the essence of my life.

YIDDISH POETS OF CANADA

Only a few are left,
Yiddish poets of Canada,
a remnant of a once mighty gathering
of Yiddish wordsmiths, singers.
In love with mother tongue, in shadow,
they kindled little flickering flames,
took pains to publish their slim volumes,
often quarreled but remained in fellowship.

Jacob-Isaac Segal walked, as was his manner,
clouded, fretting and reticent,
but laden with songs and poems
like a fruit tree heavy with fruit.
And Meleh Ravitch, pedant and dreamer,
arrived from far-away lands and continents
to find in Montreal his harbour.
Of a new Yiddish Bible he ruminated
and crowned in feverish nights
a new generation of Yiddish poets.
And Rachel Korn continued here
her luminous songs of joy and sorrow.

There were other poets, too:
The self-effacing Moshe Schaffir,
Abram Shkolnikov, Esther Segal, Ida Maze.
Gentle, motherly were Ida's poems,
her home was always open, welcoming.
In the Jewish Library on Esplanade
they gathered and celebrated
new Yiddish books of verse and prose
and enhanced the world with their own lines.

I'll not pass by the poet Sholem Stern,
crusader for peace and social justice,
who depicted the trials and tribulations
of the greenhorn newcomers in Montreal;
or his younger brother, pen-named Ish-Yoir,
steeped in Cabala, seminal in each line;
or Noah Gotlieb who exchanged the poverty of
Lithuania
for his meager Montreal existence.
Frail and unassuming, he authored many books,
let his wife promote them all over the town.

And what about Shapse Pearl or Mirel Shatan,
one volume authors who lived in shadow
of their more prominent comrades.
When the luminaries from New York came by –
Leivick, Leyeles, Reisen, Opatoshu –
they drank their words with eager reverence.

Soon from overseas arrived a remnant
from Europe's death camps, ghetto flames,
each one with his woe and dried tears.
Taciturn in his pain was Joseph Rogel,
And Chava Rosenfarb began to sing with zest
the ballad of her gutted Jewish nest.
And Peretz Miransky, like a pomegranate
full of brilliant fables and lyrics;
and Isaac Goldkorn, a rebel, with sharp epigrams
he unmasked hypocrisies and falsehoods;
and Mordechai Husid, in both Jewish tongues
proficient,
immersed in mystical, holy acronyms.

Did I leave someone out? Shlomo Mitzmacher or
Miriam Krant,
both faithful denizens of Yiddish land.
And in Toronto: Yudika, Nisenevitch and Nepom,
proletarian poets of need and strife.
A glorious page of Yiddish poetry
with heart and soul they inscribed.

O Yiddish poets of Canada,
one by one you have passed on, all forgotten,
leaving behind a treasure trove
to be discovered and admired.

MORRIS ROSENFELD

He had a child, a sunny little boy,
but seldom could he be with him:
The child was sleeping when he left
and was asleep when he returned,
only night released the father
from his daily drudgery.

He then sang the gloomy song
of all downcast fathers
and their disappointed children,
the hard song of a grey existence:
Az och un vey! Only bread and tea,
only the humming of machines
in the steaming sweatshop.

Like hidden flames his words
burst in rebellious song,
damning the mighty of this world!

But despair did not subdue
the poet's heart into submission.
He carried anew and again,
for his fellow workingmen –
songs of courage and consolation.

SHOLOM ASCH

It's not so long since he was striving,
so young, so free and undaunted,
in Jewish towns of Poland
or on sidewalks of great cities,
attuned to the joy of his people,
and their need and powerlessness.

Who depicted more keenly
our dwellings on Vistula's shores?
Portrayed our graceful daughters,
the mothers with the Shechina bonnets,
and lit our narrow ghetto panes
with the gleam of kindled Sabbath lights?

From Kutno to New York,
over oceans and world wide roads,
resounded, out of his opuses,
his exalted song of Jew and Man.

Though many took great pain
to estrange and exile him,
forever he'll remain in our midst.

YOUR POEMS

In memory of Moshe Shulshtein

I read today your poems –
hearty and courageous,
sad and bleeding
poems.

Like a shadow I follow you
in a faraway city
where danger lurked at you
from all sides.

I shared your joy and grief,
put on the yellow badge you wore
and the woe from your lines
embraced me and consoled,
pained and caressed –
my unfamiliar brother,
Yiddish poet.

It seems to be our common fate
to be driven and lashed
by cloudbursts and whirlwinds.
But whole and strong
must remain our song,
able to withstand the hatred
of all the shriveled hearts,
denying life, denying humankind!

MY ODYSSEY

At the feet of wise men I sat
and drank their words of wisdom
like from a deep well,
to quench the thirst of my soul.

I swallowed their printed words
till midnight and dawn;
sparks of light and faith
I struck out of them.

Time passed swiftly, the years
and seasons alternated;
the burden of man-and-Jew
weighed heavily upon my shoulders.

Now I return – an Odysseus
from far-away enchanted places,
over islands and seas I travelled,
tested by sorcerers and cyclops.

I've gathered and carry in me
treasures of love and light –
Isaiah's and Amos' prophesies,
the utterings of Nazarene;

The blind bard's hexameters,
Job's woeful lament,
the wisdom of Confucius,
Buddha's healing smile.

This I carry in me
in this late hour of life,
back to the shrunken assembly
of greyheaded Yiddish poets.

JULIAN TUWIM

Juliam Tuwim,
what angel or demon
transfigured you,
a prophetic Jew –
into a Polish poet.

You were a meteor
that illumined Poland's horizon.
Before your light extinguished
you left a monument
for epochs and generations.

Rash and restless you were,
in just and angry outburst
you lashed with a fiery rod
the rich and mighty
but sunshined the want
that dwells in basements and attics.

You ploughed deeply in the ground
of the people's language and life
that your words may come up
like the sunburned ears of corn
over Polish fields and meadows;
the galipot of oaks should flow in them,
the fragrance of mowed hay
after a refreshing summer rain.
You were an alchemist of words,
overturned and orchestrated them.
Amazed were all, they pointed fingers,
"Who is he, the sorcerer-singer?"

Who were you indeed? Disclose now
when your flesh is dust and your blood
runs in the lines of your poems.
What were you dreaming on lonely nights,
in cafes at daytime,
what were you mulling?
Did you hear the call of blood
of your eternal stem?
Where you pulled, on home ground,
towards Jews with earlocks and beards
or to the young Jewish hotheads?

Only in exile, on foreign soil
when Polish Jews were hacked and burned
(among them your own mother),
you opened wide window and door
and raised such a hue and cry,
"We Polish Jews –
Beilises, gudlayes,
despised, hunted quarry."

You returned to Poland
with a cherished dream:
to witness once more a Polish spring
and rest in a coffin of Polish pine.

In my mind I see your tombstone
with fiery letters inscribed,
"Here lies the bard of Poland,
a Jew by birth and pain."

MICHELANGELO

A giant among men, he wrestled
with the angel of harmony and beauty
and out of stone and marble charmed
graceful body lines and curves.

Day and night, lying on the scaffolds,
he enlivened the Sistine Chapel
with a Song of Songs to the Almighty
and his chosen race on earth.

To the last he did not relinquish
his brush from those veined hands,
until he had completed his triumphant,
apocalyptic, glorious "Last Judgment".

VAN GOGH

Drunk with light and love for life,
in open field, under the glaring sun,
Van Gogh paints his landscapes
with steady hand, hurriedly running
his brush over the canvas.
A prisoner of light and shadow,
exaltation and bottomless despair.

THE HULEH VALLEY

The *Huleh Valley*, in gaudy colours,
mirrors itself in clear fish ponds.
The golden sheaves of wheat and corn
bend in wind like in Joseph's dream.
A tractor moves slowly and hums
the song of Galileean settlements
redeemed from the poisonous swamps.

The Jordan flows here quietly
as if in itself absorbed,
until awakened by boisterous voices
from Kibbutz Amir's amphitheatre
where Sholem Aleichem's Tevye the Dairyman
is staged.

Far and wide resounds the rustic laughter
of young Galilean kibbutzniks,
as far as the muted Mount of Naftali,
over the ridges of the Golan Heights.

Above, the firmament is jewelled
with stars – guardians of life and renewal.

KLEZMERS

Melodies, hearty tunes
played by young *klezmers*
pluck the heartstrings, revive
the memory of Jewish shtetls
erased from the face of the earth.
Engagements, weddings, circumcisions
reappear from deep forgetfulness,
waiters, jesters, *mitzvah-dances*,
Purim shpils and joyful *hakofes*.

Play, young *klezmers*, play
melodies long forgotten;
conjure Jewish folk tunes,
happy, familiar, dances.
Let the violin's bow quiver
with blissful Yiddish motifs.

Let the music resound wide and far,
because whatever – Jews we are.

III.
MY SONG

MY SONG

To the flyer who roams above the land,
to the miner who descends underground –
my praise.

To all who grieve in our midst,
to the whore who walks the streets –
my greetings.

To the stricken one, chained to his chair,
to one in silent prayer –
my solace.

To man, in God's image created,
downtrodden and humiliated –
my song.

WONDERFUL CITY

You won't cover up,
Wonderful City,
with your boulevards and palaces
the poverty
that nests in back alleys,
rooming houses, attics,
where people languish
in loneliness, in filth.

And you will not redeem,
Wonderful City,
with your galleries and statues
the shame of streetwalkers
who on this April day
wait for anyone to profane
their young, holy bodies.

IN THE AMPHITEATRE

Under the night's blue firmament
dark green trees surround
the Zuckerman Amphiteatre,
Earl Bales Park, Toronto.
A semi-circle of seats
slope symmetrically downward.
There, at centre stage,
"The Taming of the Shrew"
is acted out.

The air, tart with the scent
of mowed grass and greenery,
woven by playful winds.
On the sage, down below,
resound the boisterous voices
of bold Petruccio and lively Kate.
Above the audience acknowledges
the young actors and their leader
with bravos and standing ovation,
on a quiet July night
adorned with silvery stars.

BOOK OF PSALMS

When I return home exhausted
and lie down on my couch in the corner,
I open the Psalms of David,
who was hunted, exiled
by his numerous adversaries.
Then my heart begins to melt:
How the anger of the wicked
still sears the life of the just and meek!

I find myself murmuring into the Psalm-book:
"Like you, King David, I am afflicted
and crowned with the thorns of suffering.
Like you I wander over lands and cities,
fleeing from the rage of evildoers
who cut off my stem and branches
with not one thought of mercy or regret."

WORMWOOD AND HONEY

Wormwood and honey – life's familiar potion,
pain and joy provided with generous hand;
dark cloudbursts and sudden sunshine,
Edens of delight and Gehenna depths …

This you prepared, for us, human beings,
and grounded it in unalterable law.
Between rapture and dejection, blasphemy and blessing
sways back and forth my bequeathed day.

LONESOME

All day I strayed
on unfamiliar streets,
caught in the prickly nets
of the autumn rain.

I felt extinguished,
searched for a spark
to fire me,
a few balmy words
that would melt my heart
frozen in its grief.

I looked for a handshake,
even one word of consolation –
and found none, nothing,
but myself to cling to.

ALONE

Without a fellow man, a friend
to exchange a word of wit,
leisure time is not well spent,
faltering is your spirit.

In the park, alone like a bird
that strayed from its cozy nest,
you walk diminished, deeply hurt,
in quietude, in hopeless quest.

The sharpening of mind on mind
like sparks that glisten in the air,
is a blessing for humankind,
it makes us amiable and fair.

Thus said the sage, wisest of all:
"Man is a social animal."

FRIENDSHIP

For Abe and Chawa Sloma

Like warm rays that embrace
trees and plants on earth's landscape,
gird them with vitality
they may rise, not falter,
so is the warmth of true friends
whose goodwill shines ever brightly,
that lifts you from your pinched little shell
into higher spheres of love and life.
And you may depend
on them succoring you
in your hour of need and trial.

REPENTANCE

His heart throbbed. With trembling lips
he petitioned: "Forgive! Forgive!
If not – undo me, erase me
from earth's boundless surface."

And He that hovers over all
heard the desperate, parched call
and turned him – an empty shell –
into a clear, distilled well.

JOB

With all afflictions You strike me, God,
leaving me wrapped in sadness day by day;
am I not a manchild like other men,
carried and caressed in a mother's arms?

With all these trials You test me, Lord,
thrown in the lion's den, in fiery blaze;
am I not from blood and flesh and bones
kneaded by Your mighty hand?

It must be this: My tear-offering pleases You,
the freezing of my blood – Your favoured song;
I am, O God, the crown of Your creation
and Your forever bleeding captive.

WINTER MELODIES

The fresh soft snow lies before my feet,
I tread upon it with compassion
like those simpletons of Chelm
who made a great effort to spare it.

The winter night around me,
mild like a white lamb,
and I – a singing simpleton
with eyes dazzled by snow-light
and a heart full of soul-light.

\+ + +

The winter morning
shone into my window
and called me: Come
admire the snow-glimmer outside,
hear the snow-crunch
under your footsteps.
The frost will temper
your limbs and your song.

SPARROWS IN WINTER

A swarm of sparrows, in snow and cold,
the evergreen – their perennial home,
they twitter such a chirping plea –
the frost should vanish, winter go away.
Then tree and bush will blossom anew
and sparrows soar high in the air,
on roof tops and on crowns of leafy trees
in a joyful cooing, a sparrow chant.
Meanwhile they endure the long winter months.
Tiny their bodies, gentle the beaks,
but snow and cold will not subdue them,
the perennial bush – their home.
Here will they build new nests,
raise the young ones, feed and train them,
and from the roof tops, crowns of leafy trees,
sing free sparrow canticles.

THE APPLE TREE

The apple tree,
veiled in red and green,
sways calmly in the wind,
bathed in sunlight,
whole within itself
and its surrounding.

O how I envy it,
me, the uprooted, heavy hearted one,
struggling just to survive
one more endless day.

IN SNOWSTORM

Snow, swirling, drifting,
silvers the trees with its glow;
frozen and slender they stand
like sentries in a row.

On frosty days they whisper
still, as if they would pray:
"It's so far-away to springtime,
so long until a sunny day!"

Sparrows upon the treetops
hop on their tiny feet,
stroking the wind-bared branches
twittering gently and sweet:

"Dear trees, precious branches,
don't give up in despair,
spring soon will return
sunshine's warmth and care."

So chirp the sparrows in winter
while the whirling breeze
decks with white snowflakes
the icy, fettered trees.

IN THE HOSPITAL

On the fifth floor of the hospital
he lies sunken in deep distress,
face caved in, darkened,
eyes shut, with open mouth,
breathing heavily, raving
from body heat and morphine.

By his side his wife, thin and shriveled,
arranges the pillow at his head,
freshens his lips with a few drops of juice,
and looks on, hour after hour,
as he vanishes before her eyes.

At night she returns to the empty house.
The bed is cold, the sleepless night long;
her man of fifty years, left back there
on the fifth floor of the hospital.

IT WILL PASS

It will pass –
the anguish and the joy
in serene mornings, nights of inclement weather,
all the days and hours trickled, seeped,
freed from sense and senselessness.
It will pass –
the destined hour will strike
no matter if you embrace it willingly
or bewail the unfulfilled dreams
that dissolved like snow in sunlight.

Adieu –
life's vast and brilliant panorama,
hours of solitude and togetherness,
nights of sated love,
days of doubt and rejection;
memories of a home
that vanished in a cloud of fire,
and regrets, supplications –
that the earth go on thriving
with life and love forever.

THEN

O nothing will then be of any use
when your eyes will close forever,
see no more the blue light of the sky,
the shapely figures of women moving by.
You will no more revel in leisure time
with sounds of music or poetic rhyme.
The glitter of each heavenly star
will no more lure you from afar –
when you will come to eternal rest.
then know: You are temporal, a guest
to relish in life's music, its beat
at home and on tumultuous street,
to feel the warmth of sunbeams that enfold
the earth and all creatures of this world,
to sing loud paeans to ongoing life –
until your fated hour arrives.

THERE WAS A MAN

Skimpy, meagre years of life
in constant struggle for existence;
all days lead to the dank pit –
an eternal resting place.

All days with grief interwoven
in life's fabric, undivided;
short the sunlight of a life span,
long the darkness of four cubits.

Unmerciful Time, adversary
of all breathing creatures;
the whole globe – your abattoir,
Death – you refined instrument.

Who decreed such a fate,
everlasting in time and space,
silent like the circling planets,
angry like the ocean's foam?

I will sit on the ground, bewailing
the scanty days that disappear,
the numbered years that vanish,
leaving no trace on earth.

On a boulder upon a mountain
I would chisel a Man's name;
he was here, rejoiced and suffered,
Time has swallowed him. He is no more.

WITH MY LITTLE ONE

With my little one, beloved one,
in our warm and cozy tent,
I mirror myself in her eyes
like in two shining pools.

I warm myself and I nestle
in her clear and silken form
and whisper gently in her ear:
"True delight of my life!"

Outside winds roam about
over our fragile tent,
inside love and rapture
spread their wings over us.

Lord of all endless worlds,
guardian of eternity,
in an hour of grace you have granted us
handfuls of pure joy.

I embrace your lovely body,
my dear and precious one;
let the wine of love flow freely
and the honey from your mouth.

MY LITTLE GRANDSON

My little grandson, sweet and lively,
fills with joy this heart of mine;
his pure innocence permeates me
like healing rays of sunshine.

All my sadness dissipates
like a cloud in morning light
as I watch him on his tiny tractor
riding proudly like a little knight.

Soon alighted, he is circling
the room in joyful ecstasy,
until I spread out my arms
and embrace him lovingly.

Life upon you, little grandson,
of my old age – a shining crown.

YES, I DO BELIEVE

Yes, I do believe, I affirm my faith
in days to come that will uplift humankind
from the vales of tears and misery,
when the sun of freedom will shine for all,
and all will joyously create and sing.
Generations will be bound in a golden chain,
straightened and uplifted in body and in spirit
in a black-white-yellow brotherhood.
Pious and freethinkers, agnostics, men and women,
will celebrate in unison, trust each other.
Languages and cultures will bloom and prosper,
humans like the angels, mortal gods.
Heroes will arise, not in Cain-slaughter,
but eager for knowledge and sensible deeds.
The earth will provide abundantly,
the seas and rivers will be multiplied
with fish and birds above of all kind.
A new reality will dawn, an earthly Eden
of life and love, healing and forgiveness.
Poets will express and sing of this felicity –
yes, I do believe, I affirm my steadfast faith.

GLOSSARY

Yom Kippur – Day of forgivness, atonement and fasting
Yahrzeit – Memorial day after a deceased person
Tallis – Prayer shawl
Al Chet – Confessional prayer recited on Yom Kippur
Nigun – A tune, without words
Rebbe – Hasidic rabbi
Shaddai – The Almighty
Kaddish – Memorial prayer for the deceased
Ola Boga – Polish, cry for God's help
Gevald – Yiddish, cry of violence and emergency
Otwock (Otvotsk) – Resort town, 28 kilometres south of Warsaw
Shomrim – Members of the Zionist youth organization "Hashomer Hatsair"
Bundist – Members of the "Bund," a Jewish socialist party in Poland
Negev – Southern part of Israel
Az och un vey – Yiddish, alas and alack!
Baal Shem – Rabbi Israel, master of the good name, founder of Hasidism
Sechina bonnets – Headgear worn by pious women
Beilises – After Mendel Beilis, accused of ritual murder in Kiev, 1913
Huleh Valley – Swampy area in northern Israel
Klezmers – Traditional Jewish musicians
Mitzvah dances – Special dance on weddings and other Jewish celebrations
Purim shpils – Humorous playlets performed on the holiday of Purim
Hakofes – Circular procession with Torah scrolls on the last day of the holiday of the Tabernacles